30 Days

30 Days

A Devotional Memoir

D.M. WEBB

Ambassador International
GREENVILLE, SOUTH CAROLINA & BELFAST, NORTHERN IRELAND
www.ambassador-international.com

30 Days
A Devotional Memoir

ISBN: 978-1-62020-247-0
eISBN: 978-1-62020-346-0

Unless otherwise indicated, Scripture taken from the King James Version of the Holy Bible. Public Domain.

Cover design and typesetting: Matthew Mulder
E-book conversion: Anna Riebe

AMBASSADOR INTERNATIONAL
Emerald House
427 Wade Hampton Blvd.
Greenville, SC 29609, USA
www.ambassador-international.com

AMBASSADOR BOOKS
The Mount
2 Woodstock Link
Belfast, BT6 8DD, Northern Ireland, UK
www.ambassadormedia.co.uk

The colophon is a trademark of Ambassador

DEDICATIONS

First and Foremost, Thank You, Lord, for the words You put into my head and the trials and blessings that have rained down upon me. I lean upon Your continual guidance.

To Nathan: I would have waited a thousand years for you. God has blessed me with your love.

To Caleb and Blake: your love and devotion have been my buoy in the storms.

To Mom: you guided me and molded me into who I am today. I forever cherish your wisdom (and our Scrabble games).

Table of Contents

FOREWORD

THE COMPILATION OF THIS BOOK was not an easy thing for me. More or less three years in the making, through personal journals and a personal blog, each story revealed a little more about myself than I really wanted known.

I never wanted to talk about my late husband, my father, the trials I endured or the thoughts of hopelessness, loneliness, failure, and doubt. Truly, I only wanted to show the happy, sparkly times in my life.

As with all good intentions, it only matters when it is God's intention being done. I sat for so many weeks, staring at my words in my latest novel, wondering why I couldn't write, why the words wouldn't come. I knew what I wanted to say, knew what I wanted to create, but nothing happened.

Instead, my journal and blog posts kept distracting me. Books were distracting me. Finally, I sat down and printed out those blogs. I fiddled with a few of them, and then set it aside.

I tried to ignore it. Days passed and still those pages called. More days passed.

I eventually gave up the fight. Once I sat down, I edited, rearranged, and added to the stories until my eyes blurred, and yet I still pushed forward. It had to be done. I felt it in my soul.

Self-doubt and fear of utter failure would beat at me, and still I kept writing and typing. Three days later I beheld my product: three years of a spiritual journey condensed into thirty days—thirty days of stories that bared my heart and soul, my shortcomings and dreams.

It isn't that I wanted to reveal myself to others; but if what I spoke about could help others deal with similar issues, then I had tell my stories. I hope it will encourage others. I hope it will help others. Most of all, I hope it brings glory to God's name.

Day One

LIVE BY FAITH

Ask, and it shall be given you; seek, and ye shall find;
knock, and it shall be opened unto you.

Matthew 7:7

AS I WALK IN FELLOWSHIP with the Lord, He is so wonderful and does such wonderful things that at times I cannot and do not understand what He is doing. And I ask, "Why?"

My husband died eight years ago. He was a firefighter; as he responded to a house fire, his tanker truck rolled over, killing him instantly. I was numb for weeks afterward. But I did not question why. Then, barely two months later, my father died suddenly. A massive heart attack claimed his life, and I watched him leave this world. On that cold January night on that cold bathroom floor, neither I, my brother-in-law, nor the medical responders could bring him back to life.

For years I prided myself for never asking why. I believed my faith was so strong that I did not need to know why—only to accept that God knew best.

Years passed, and I knew I had lied to myself. I was hurting inside, emotions tearing at me and ripping my soul. On the outside, I was remote and tranquil.

It was then I asked why. Why was my husband taken so suddenly, and I left with two children to raise by myself? Why was the one man, whom I trusted completely and wholly, taken from this world? Why was my father taken from us? I believed I needed my father here with me; I wanted his guidance. It was his hand on my head that day that sheltered and calmed me when I received the news of Jimmy's death. It was his smile and laugh that bolstered my spirits to keep trying.

Ever heard that song "Daddy's Hands"? That was my father. Ever heard that song "When You Say Nothing at All"? That was Jimmy.

Whom could I call upon to fix that leaky pipe? Who would air my flat tire for me or patch the hole in it? Who would bush-hog my land for me? Who would fix that missing shingle on my roof or level my front door for me?

Where was my father to help me? Where was my father with whom to sit in his workshop and talk, enjoying a glass of iced tea? Why did this happen?

But as I asked that question, I learned that it was so my family could grow.

"Grow?" I asked God.

"Grow in My love," came the answer.

I learned to air that flat tire. I learned how to level that door and fix that leaky pipe. And I learned how to ask why and to ask my Lord for help in understanding His words and ways. I learned that I can still sit, with a glass of iced tea in my hand, and talk to my Heavenly Father.

Asking why is not a revelation of my lack of faith, but a testimony that my trust is in Him and my hand is held in his as He leads me through the darkness and into the light. I should not pretend that I have accepted God's ways and am walking in submission to Him when I have questions tearing at me deep inside.

God wants me to be completely honest with Him. And He promises, "Call unto Me, and I will answer thee, and shew thee great and mighty things, which thou knowest not" (Jeremiah 33:3).

My life can be a storm, as can my emotions, pitching here and there, heaving the waves, and slapping them against barriers. I love thunderstorms, but I eventually long for the calmness of the autumn days. So when these storms in my life roll and roar, one verse comes to me over and over, calming my mind and allowing me to feel His presence: "And he arose, and rebuked the wind, and said unto the sea, Peace, be still. And the wind ceased, and there was a great calm" (Mark 4:39).

Day Two

DISASTERS

*Be careful for nothing; but in everything by prayer and sup-
plication with thanksgiving let your requests be made known
unto God.*

Philippians 4:6

AS I PREPARED FOR A writer's conference one year, I learned
that there were many things to prepare: one-sheets, "elevator pitch",
business cards, synopsis, etc. And I discovered making a one-sheet
to spout my book was not easy.

I laugh at myself now. Haughty me thought I could slap it together, throw a little creativity into it, and make it look good. I
silently chided myself.

It looked amateurish. It looked pathetic. Now I know not to
take shortcuts under any circumstances. I doled out a little cash
and bought a small software program designed to create all that
I needed.

Being creative was one thing, but without the proper tools, the project looked plain. The story written is an author's brainchild. If I had put so much time in writing, tacking together the perfect words, laboring well into the night, should I not put the extra effort into making the selling tools for that story as wonderful as I could? My design wasn't flawed—it was the media I used.

Just as writing and design programs were the physical media for success, so prayer was the spiritual medium for success. In fact, I learned prayer was the most effective medium out there.

I prayed that my dream would come true. I prayed that my trip would be safe. I prayed for calmness. Most importantly, I prayed that God's will be done.

Sometimes I applied the wrong medium, and the results were disastrous or amateurish; but, once I went back to the beginning and applied the right program, the right medium, the right prayer, that was when marvelous things began to happen.

Even if my life was held together by spit, barbed wire, duct tape, and prayer, I learned prayer is the strongest medium there is. And I'm a "work in progress," Lord.

Day Three

ISAIAH AND DANIEL

The Lord God is my strength . . .

Habakkuk 3:19

ISAIAH AND DANIEL—WHAT DO THESE two books have in common? Both are prophetic. Both are referenced time and time again. And both carry passages to which a firefighter can relate.

I read a book by an exceptional writer whose character was a firefighter. Midway through the book the character read a passage from *Isaiah 43:2*: "When you pass through the waters, I will be with you; and through the rivers, they shall not overflow you. When you walk through the fire, you shall not be burned, nor shall the flame scorch you."

How true. It did not need to be the fire that raged and consumed a house or a forest, but the fire that raged in my life. I could pass through the fire without being burned as long as I had Him by my side.

When the book ended, it had a passage from *Daniel 3:24-25*: "Then Nebuchadnezzar the king was astonied, and rose up in haste, and spake, and said unto his counsellors, Did not we cast three men bound into the midst of the fire? They answered and said unto the king, True, O king. He answered and said, Lo, I see four men loose, walking in the midst of the fire, and they have no hurt; and the form of the fourth is like the Son of God.'"

That passage was something my husband, a firefighter, taught during opening assembly every two months. Jimmy once told me a story about his training and the smoke house. To simulate a fire, a house would be flooded with smoke, and the firefighters would have to learn to navigate by feel. Jimmy ended up separated from his team. It was a scary situation. Unknown to them, there was always a trainer nearby to pull them out in case of an emergency.

Imagine: they could not see in front of them. They used hands on shoulders, on walls, and feeling along the hose to navigate through the smoke. Their air tanks only had so long before the alarm sounded, indicating low levels. Jimmy was frightened, and his tank was running low. His two teammates had been enveloped by the black smoke—and Jimmy was alone. The passage in *Daniel* came to mind. Then he saw a form in front of him that helped guide him to safety. Was it the trainer? Was it the Lord?

Afterward he found out that the trainers were on the other side of the house, and no one was remotely close to Jimmy. The Lord guided him because he called upon His name.

I kept that story close to my heart because it never failed to remind me that the Lord is always near; and, when I call upon

His name, His strength is there to guide and protect. I can walk the fire of life—I have Him at my side.

Day Four

I DON'T LOVE
YOU ENOUGH

And now abideth faith, hope, charity, these three;
but the greatest of these is charity.

1 Corinthians 13:13

MY MOTHER AND I HAD an interesting conversation one day. What she said was profound, and it left me with the knowledge that I did not understand the capacity of God's love.

It all began with the story of doing for others and for your neighbors. If her friend or neighbor came to her house for a cup of sugar, she would give that neighbor two cups of sugar. When the friend needed something that she could spare, she would give that person twice as much as she was asking. Why? That's because when it was given with love, blessings abounded. Mom always said she would like to have friends owing her favors. That way when she died, she would die laughing, because they would never be able to repay the favors.

One year, at a mission camp, she was led to stand and give a testimony. She thought it was just going to be a "thank you for everyone here, yadda, yadda, yadda." Even though the sentence "Please let me hurry up and get off the stage" repeated in her mind, she spoke and later could not remember even half of what she said.

As she spoke her testimony turned to sacrifices. "I am no Abraham," she said. Line her children up or her grandchildren, and say that she must choose one to sacrifice, even if it meant saving her own soul or someone else's, and she would say, "No."

She loves all her children equally—even though we drive her half crazy—and she loves her grandchildren equally. How could she decide among her artist (me), her drama queen (my sister), and her beloved son (my brother)? How could she decide among her prayer warrior (my oldest son), her little man (my youngest son), her friend (my nephew), her princess (my niece), her captain (my youngest nephew), or the baby (my youngest niece)?

She could not choose because she could not love *anyone* enough to sacrifice her own child or grandchild. She does not love her sisters that much. She does not love her brothers that much. She does not love her neighbors that much. She does not love her church family that much. Why would she sacrifice a part of herself for them?

Why would I?

But God did.

He loved everyone *so much* that He gave His only Son for us. I have to say that again: He sacrificed His only Son for *us*!

Can you imagine that love? I really cannot. I cannot imagine loving someone so much that I would sacrifice my son for him.

But God did.

I do not believe that anyone can comprehend the extent and the expanse of God's love for us. And if He loves me so much, then why do I at times turn away from Him? Why do I not run into His arms and live the life He wishes for me to have?

Why do people not accept the gift of His sacrificed Son? I am glad I accepted the gift He gave me, even though I cannot understand the greatness, the simplicity, the vastness of His love for me.

"For God so loved the world, that He gave His only begotten Son, that whosoever believeth in Him shall not perish, but have everlasting life" (John 3:16).

Day Five

PEACE, BE STILL

Grace to you and peace from God our Father, and the Lord Jesus Christ.

Romans 1:7

ONE SUNDAY MORNING AT A writer's conference, just a few moments away from breakfast, I ducked into the prayer room. I had not visited this room until then. Lying on the table, opened to me, was a Bible that someone had left for prayer room use. I flipped pages, scanned passages, and somewhere within the depths of my heart a voice urged me onward. So I flipped more pages, scanned more passages, until I came to a rest at *Mark 4:39*. "And he arose, and rebuked the wind, and said unto the sea, 'Peace, be still.' And the wind ceased, and there was a great calm."

Many versions have different words, but they all mean the same. Peace = hush = quiet. In that small room, sitting on that hard metal chair, comfortable and quiet, I knew that day my mind was to stay quiet.

Most times my mind would race from one thought to the next, one scenario to another, one imagining to the following, and even one dream back to reality. That day, my mind no longer held thoughts, scenarios, imaginings or dreams. That day, I sat and listened; I sat and talked—and I did not let my mind wander.

"Peace, be still" echoed throughout me.

My heart shone with an inner light, and it beat as one with an inner song. That day I realized that even though I gave myself to the Lord many, many years ago, I was now living for Him. The storms within me quieted, and the sea of my heart and mind calmed.

I saw things that I knew would be part of my future. I saw ideas that sprang forth. I saw roads open before me. Like that steady beat of a caravan's drum, I marched to the endlessly pounding and comforting beat, slow, steady, and yet still, even though I knew the road would be long, dusty at times, and oftentimes stormy.

When I came home, I brought that peace with me. It reached out and laid its hands on my sons. One day after I came home, my youngest son arose, and he opened the Bible and read from *Ecclesiastes 3:1-8*: "To everything there is a season . . . " and then he read *John 3:16*. I stood at the stove, bacon popping and the waffle iron steaming, lost in the words he was reading.

Blake never read; he hated it. But there at our small, scuffed, and worn table, he read. He read with such an understanding, one that I had never seen in a nine-year-old.

From all the storms that haunted our lives and from all the hatred that abounded throughout the world and was broadcast on the news, the peace in that one little room shielded us—and continues to do so today.

Day Six

PUTTING IT ALL INTO PERSPECTIVE

In the beginning God created the heaven and the earth.

Genesis 1:1

GOD KNOWS MY DESIRES AND dreams. Did He not say, "Ask and it shall be given"? Did He not say He will fulfill the desire of my heart? Yes—as long as I ask for it the right way.

I asked Him, "Please let the stories You have placed in my heart reach the readers who thirst for them." He knew I have always, since the time I was a young girl, wanted to be either an astronaut or a writer. The writer side won, but the side that saw the stars at night helped me to see things in perspective.

Observe: the Earth's diameter is 7,926 miles. The sun's diameter is 864,900 miles. In comparison, Jupiter has a diameter of 88,846 miles. Since one light year is 5.9 trillion miles (5,900,000,000,000), the solar system is calculated to be around 3.2 light years in diameter. That is 3.2 multiplied by 5.9 trillion miles which looks like this: 188,800,000,000,000 miles. Our solar system is part of the Milky Way galaxy, whose diameter is approximately 100,000 light years; that is 100,000 multiplied by 5.9 trillion miles which looks like this: 590,000,000,000,000,000 miles. This is beyond a trillion. Of course our Milky Way galaxy is part of a super cluster that contains thousands of major galaxies and countless smaller ones. This super cluster is approximately tens of millions of light years (multiply that number by 5,900,000,000,000). This is a number I cannot even name, but God can.

Here is another fast fact: a paraphrase from a science book that actually proves that God exists, because physics is a constant and science is supposed to explain other than saying a "super force."

The Big Bang was not an explosion as we think of it—it was an explosion of space and the beginning of time. The theory cannot explain what came before. All that can be said is that the universe was infinitely small and extremely hot as it came into being. For the first 10^{-43} seconds—called "Planck time"—the normal laws of physics did not apply.

Inflation—a sudden expansion in the first instant of creation, during which the universe grew from tinier than an atom to bigger than a galaxy—was needed to explain the universe today. The best suggestion as to what caused this growth was that huge amounts of energy were released as forces were separated from a unified super force.

My take on this is that physics always apply, but God makes exceptions, since He wrote the rulebook on physics.

Compared to the vastness of our "little" neighborhood, Earth is insignificant in comparison. So why should I dwell on the small details of life? I shouldn't.

The God who created a universe so vast that I can't even measure it is also the God who will have my dreams fulfilled when He wants them to be fulfilled.

All in His time and in His way: having this little perspective on life helped in knowing that all is under control, as long as I follow Him.

The God who created the vast universe down to the little fishes in the sea—He's the God who cares about me.

Day Seven

THE PASSION OF THE CHRIST

And he said unto Jesus, Lord, remember me
when thou comest unto thy kingdom.

Luke 23:42

MANY PEOPLE HAVE SEEN THE movie *The Passion of the Christ*, and many have cast it off while others hold it dear. I hold it dear. I cannot watch it without being reminded of the sacrifice that was given for little, unworthy me.

Some people would say, "I do not need to be reminded. I know that Christ died for us." And I would reply, "Yes, you and everyone need to be reminded every once in a while just how much Christ suffered for us." I know I need to be reminded.

Pictures I have seen show this glamorous man on a cross, with nary a trace of blood on Him. Some show a man with a look of acceptance on His face. I don't buy that.

Christ suffered horribly. Even though I knew that this was just a movie, it held true to form for that time period. They had scourged Him, flaying the skin from His body. They beat Him, slapped and punched Him, tripped Him, chained Him. They drove that crown of thorns deep into His head.

Blood would have been dripping from Him, leaving a trail all the way to the hill. Weariness would have set in. He would have looked on the people who yelled. Why do this for the people who spat on Him, who cursed Him, who ripped His flesh from His body?

He would have felt great pain watching His disciples scatter and knowing that His faithful disciples, His beloved friends, had denied Him. Once on the cross, His hands nailed down, shoulders pulled out, feet nailed, and pain coursing through His body, He would have felt abandoned by His Father because He carried all the weight of the world's sins: murder, adultery, fornication, stealing, coveting, blasphemy, etc., was upon Him.

Only a handful of friends were there, and even then did the true impact of what He was doing reach them at all? I would like to think so. Jesus had His body ripped, torn, bloodied, beaten, and nailed for every unworthy creature on this earth because He thinks we are worthy.

Tears poured down my face, my heart was lightened, and my soul was cleansed when I realized that Jesus laid His life down for all of us, taking the brunt of evil and shielding us for all time because we are His and to Him we are worthy of saving.

It makes me humble to know that I am His. I will not have to suffer eternal separation because He already suffered for me. And like the thief on the cross, I will be in paradise with my Lord when I leave this earth.

Day Eight

DISCOVERY

Blessed are they that mourn, for they shall be comforted.

Matthew 5:4

I BELIEVE THERE ARE MANY books besides the Bible that Christians should read, books that can be contemplated over and over again. I read a page or two and then stop, mulling over what I just read and what just spoke to my heart.

I once read a book titled *The Search for Significance* by Robert S. McGhee.

Do I harbor resentment within me? Do I consider myself a failure or unloveable? Maybe I did harbor a little more resentment than I realized. I did, deep down within me, consider myself unloveable and a failure, destined for rejection. It was a harsh realization. That little grain of sand within me wanted to throw the book away for this revelation, but the yearning within me to grow closer to God crushed it to my bosom, hugging the truth.

"When the light of love and honesty shines on the thoughts of hopelessness, it is often painful. We begin to admit that we really do feel negatively about ourselves—and have for a long time" (McGhee 2003, 6).

As I thought about what I read, I knew this: I was afraid that I was unloveable and would be rejected. I had had a failed marriage, lost a child, lost my grandmother, become a widow, lost my father, and then lost a beloved aunt and another grandmother, and was no longer receiving love from my family (or so I had thought)—all this in a ten-year span. I was bashed and beaten down for believing in the dream of being an author. For many of those ten years I was a piece of flotsam swirling around in the frothing, rushing waters. I had nothing to stand on, nothing that gave me peace. I had a pastor friend, and then I didn't. The church split, I left, he left, and a friendship died. I had lost a friend when I desperately needed one. Then came a wrong relationship that damaged me further than I thought possible.

Resentment at the failed married, the loss of loved ones, arrows of hatred aimed at me, and the loss of people I depended on caused me to feel unloved and a failure. It all seemed to be my fault. I was the one to blame, because I could not be who they wanted me to be.

But now that I see the horrible truth, I know this: I am not a failure to God. He knows my heart and my continuing attempt to do His will and learn from His words. I am loved. I am not rejected in God's eyes. I may be different, but God loves me.

As long as I stay true to the Lord and follow Him, my life will be enriched. I am blessed.

Day Nine

BING AND BAM

For I know the thoughts that I think towards you, saith the Lord, thoughts of peace, and not of evil, to give you an expected end.

Jeremiah 29:11

I HAVE READ AND HEARD people say they had a sudden "epiphany." I didn't really like that word. It made me think of something itsy, bitsy, teeny, weenie—barely a grape nut of an idea. Even pronouncing the word makes it seem small. I like the word "revelation." Epiphany is the little Edison bulb—bing!—the light comes on. Revelation is the Emeril Lagasse BAM! It's the supernova of an exploding idea so bright it leaves only a word to be said: oi!

My "oi" moment came while mowing the yard one day. Maybe to some it was a chore, but I found being on my riding lawn mower a relaxing time that I spent with God. I happily chugged along whacking the grass down to non-jungle depths, and my mind floated around in silent conversation.

Most times it was only a gentle prodding or a small nudge of a thought. Something that made me go "hmm." Then, like that day, BAM! I just about fell off the mobile mechanical cow.

During the fall, I had the chance to hire someone to bush-hog the part of the land that escaped cutting (*i.e.*, the lawn mower broke and "things" grew back). By having it bush-hogged, I was able to cut a section of the land I called "The Grove". I could admire its beauty. I found a place that would be nice for a hammock. There was a place that needed thinning. And I discovered where the rain took my Bermuda grass seeds. So while I was cutting, the "oi" moment came to me.

Why did I expect to do all my "yard decorating" and planting at one time? Why did I keep expecting to do everything at once? God took six days to create everything. How am I any better?

I'm not. Because of my imperfection, it would take me longer— much, much longer—to "fix up" the land to my ideals; but I could enjoy the natural beauty that I was able to finally appreciate since the dratted jungle was cut down to size.

As I planned and conceived ideas for building this or removing that, I trucked along on my eager-to-consume-grass lawn mower, having my conversation with God, and enjoying the beauty of nature. It would take time to do all that I want, and better yet, it would be in His own timing.

Day Ten

FEAR AND DREAMS

But Jesus beheld them, and said unto them, "With men this is impossible; but with God all things are possible."

Matthew 19:26

MANY TIMES I PLANNED THINGS, had dreams. I worked and strived to make those plans or dreams a reality. As someone close to me pointed out in *Proverbs 16:3*, "Commit thy works unto the Lord, and thy thoughts shall be established."

I realized I had not turned over my dreams and thoughts to the Lord. Why didn't I? It's because I still harbored fear in my heart—fear of being alone; fear of not having my dreams realized; fear of having my heart torn apart; fear of not having what I desired; fear of actually having my dreams come to fruition, but having to stand alone.

Another snippet of wisdom was once told to me: fear kills everything.

I don't remember who said that to me, but it stuck with me for a long time.

So how did I overcome this kind of fear? I laid it at the cross. The Lord knew my desires, my dreams, my longings. Once I had faith and turned it over to Him, I realized that all things were possible.

When I made a decision, knowing it was the hardest I ever had to make, doubts would badger my mind. Did I do the right thing? Did I make the right choice? Is this something that was meant to be? etc., etc., etc.

I don't believe in chance encounters or coincidences. Everything happens for a reason; everything has a purpose. Sometimes I don't know what that purpose may be.

Take a relationship, for example. Was there a mistake that happened that caused it to wither? Or was it fear? Fear destroys all things, as does pride—pride in "I did no wrong" or fear in "I'm not ready for this." Either or both parties can relate to this kind of doubt or fear. The difference is whether the person will fall to the dark side of doubt and fear or stand firm in faith and embrace the light.

I stood firm, but I also had the tendency to run. I stood on the edge of the shadow, back to the dark and facing the light. One step backward and I would be fully enveloped in the dark side of life: pleasure, boasting, selfishness, etc. That is the world. But if I took one huge step forward, then I would be basking in the light: joy, warmth, love, which is not of this world. The question was: would I take that step in faith and into the light or would I retreat into the known and hide in the dark?

I am not of this world.

I prefer the light. I couldn't stay in the dark. I am a child of the Light, and that is where I belong.

My prayers are for those lost in the dark to realize that the Light is nothing to be scared of. Children of Light cannot hide forever in the dark with those who are part of the world. Spots on the soul? Stains? The Light removes them.

All it took for me to be able to feel its warmth on my skin and its love in my heart was one step in faith, one step in trust.

Day Eleven

A FLIP-FLOP LIFE

Who layeth the beams of his chambers in the waters:
who maketh the clouds of his chariot: who walketh upon the wings
of the wind.

Psalm 104:3

FLIP-FLOPS: THE PERFECT WORD FOR summer—and for life, because life can be a flip-flop sometimes.

Just when I thought all the pieces were falling into place, KABOOM! A hurricane ripped them from the playing board and scattered them onto the sand. Another do-over—but that was okay. Life is full of do-overs; if not, how would I learn?

Even though life teaches me lessons, I have to remember from where the lessons come. A verse was posted online one day, a verse that I was needing on that down-and-out day.

"Wherefore let him that thinketh he standeth take heed lest he fall. There hath no temptation taken you but such as is common to man:

but God is faithful, who will not suffer you to be tempted above that you are able; but will with the temptation also make a way to escape, that ye may be able to bear it" (1 Corinthians 10:12-13).

For some people, words are just words, and sometimes I have felt the same. I have reminders each and every morning when I wake up, reminders throughout the day, and reminders each and every night as I lie down to sleep: that I must walk in faith and that Jesus is the Way, the Truth, and the Life. Even though temptations seek me, because of Him they would never conquer me.

How does life seem like a flip-flop, though? Life is full of emotions, ideals, and dreams. I keep my feet well protected from the hot sand as I would protect my heart from hot emotions. I soothe my soles with comfort as I would soothe my soul with the Lord's words. I tread carefully on the sand as I would tread carefully on my dreams. And I would watch out, because life can flip right on over.

Not only life, but love can be a flip-flop. It can run deep, hot, and all-consuming. Or it can creep on someone like the stars at night, one by one peeking down until they shine with its brilliance.

God has a perfect way for love to happen, and I shouldn't tamper with that way lest I suffer the consequences: confusion, pain, loneliness, anger, etc.

Wait upon the Lord. Peace, be still . . .

They are words to remember. Be still my heart. Keep my flip-flops on, and trust that God will see to my every desire. Unlike we humans, God never breaks His promise.

Day Twelve

EVERYTHING
HAS ITS TIME

A time to kill, and a time to heal; a time to break down,
and a time to build up;
A time to weep, and a time to laugh; a time to mourn,
and a time to dance; . . .
A time to rent, and a time to sew; a time to keep silence,
and a time to speak;
A time to love, and a time to hate; a time of war,
and a time of peace.

Ecclesiastes 3:3-4, 7-8

THIS WAS A NICE PASSAGE to read when I found myself not knowing how I felt or what to feel. What were these thoughts that bounced around in my head? What were these feelings that haunted and pierced me? What were these dreams that I saw but could not seem to obtain?

And to think that these questions were only the sprinkles on the cupcake. I had not even bitten into the cushiony inside. Would it be chocolate, devil's food, vanilla, angel's food, red velvet, or maybe even strawberry? Any choice would be a surprise.

Isn't life a surprise? Whether some believe in pre-determination or chance or free will, life still has the ability to dish out surprises whenever I round that corner. Maybe I could see it at times, there in the hazy future, or maybe it was hidden in the dark shadows as I approached.

The only down side was when I received the surprise, the gift, and I was left wondering, "What now? What's the next step?"

Not long ago, after weeks of sunshiny days, I was left bereft. I could travel that merry-go-around all I wanted, and I would never arrive at an answer, only self-doubt and more questions. That passage helped. There was a time for everything.

"A time to keep silence." It was not an easy thing to keep silent. Silence is golden, as the old saying goes. Silence gave me time to think, to recall things in retrospect, but most of all to listen—to listen to my heart, my mind, and to God. It required trust and patience.

Sometimes I believe God's answer is "patience, my child."

Day Thirteen

TREAD CAREFULLY ON MY DREAMS

*And again, I will put my trust in him. And again, Behold,
I, and the children which God hath given me.*

Hebrews 2:13

*HAD I the heavens' embroidered cloths,
Enwrought with golden and silver light,
The blue and the dim and the dark cloths
of night and light and the half-light,
I would spread the cloths under your feet:
But I, being poor, have only my dreams;
I have spread my dreams under your feet;
Tread softly because you tread on my dreams.*

W.B. Yeats

SOMETIMES I FOUND MYSELF WHERE it was only my dreams that kept me company. Every once in a while I offered my dreams to someone, and my wish was "tread softly because you tread on my dreams."

It was a fearsome thing for me to show a portion of myself. My emotions, my thoughts, my dreams were what defined my personality.

Have you ever offered a piece of yourself, lain it at the feet of someone, and wondered if it would be accepted?

Have you ever looked into a person's eyes, wished for him to see your heart, and wondered if it would be accepted?

Have you ever listened to your own heart, felt what it says, and wondered if you could accept it?

A life can parallel the teachings of Jesus.

He laid His life down for us.

He offered His love to us.

My heart cries out for *Him.*

If I trust in Him, I will always be accepted. Jesus treads carefully on my dreams.

Day Fourteen

HAVE OR HAVE NOT

Again, the kingdom of heaven is like unto a merchant man, seeking goodly pearls.

Matthew 13:45

I'M ALWAYS STRIVING TO PERFECT my craft. I study books and teachings of other authors, editors, and publishers. I had purchased one book, *The Art & Craft of Writing Christian Fiction*, by Jeff Gerke, founder of Marcher Lord Press. In it he stated, "[A]n attitude of humility before God and others will serve you well as you pursue a career in Christian fiction publishing."

To understand this, I had to define humility. Good ole' Webster defined it thus: "the quality or state of being humble." I had to define humble: not proud or haughty; not arrogant or assertive; reflecting, expressing, or offered in a spirit of deference or submission.

To be humble, I had to learn and continue to do so, and to never, ever say, "I know it all." That brought me to a quote by a famous person: "The only true wisdom consists of knowing that you know nothing." Bill S. Preston, Esquire may have said this in his excellent adventure with his friend Theodore "Ted" Logan, but it was first stated by Socrates.

No one would ever know it all, albeit most politicians and some English professors may think so. I am humble enough to know that I know nothing about writing, and yet I know how to write.

Have you ever read an author who started out so strong and vibrant, only to pick up a tenth or eleventh book and gag over the storyline? What happened to the editor? How could it be published with so many mistakes? Have you ever read a book and immediately forgot the title, the storyline, or the characters?

I don't want to be like that, so I continually learn and adapt.

The key to writing is to learn and listen, then apply.

The key to life is to learn and listen, then apply.

The key to prayer is to learn and listen, then apply.

Every pearl started out as a rough grain of sand.

Day Fifteen

GLORY IN THE HIGHEST

*And the angel said unto them, Fear not: for behold, I bring you
good tidings of great joy, which shall be to all people. For unto you
is born this day in the city of David a Saviour, which is Christ
the Lord. And this shall be a sign unto you; Ye shall find the
babe wrapped in swaddling clothes, lying in a manger. And suddenly there was with the angel a multitude of the heavenly host
praising God, and saying, Glory to God in the highest, and on
earth peace, good will towards men.*

Luke 2:10-14

NO MATTER THE AGE, NO matter how many times it is read, the
story of Christ's birth will never become old. Each year it is read
with fresh eyes and new revelations burst forth. Has anyone ever
read the Song of Mary (Luke 1:46-55)? How about the prophecy of
Simeon (Luke 2:28-35)?

Reading about the simple birth of Christ made me think of how Christmas is celebrated. Do I rush out and buy the latest techno gadget for my children? Do I lament not having the newest decorations? Do I complain about not having enough presents under the tree? Do I scurry about, trying to locate the perfect present on someone's wish list?

For the last few Christmases, an inexpensive white tree has been assembled in my home. The decorations were painted bells, old glass balls, painted ornaments, lacquered pine cones and sweet-gum balls, and childhood ornaments passed down to me. There were no presents under the tree, but when they did appear there were not many.

Why do we need a Christmas wish list? A gift is something given, and normally something that is a surprise. If it comes from a wish list, where is the surprise, the love of giving? A wish list becomes the obligation list.

My gifts were what I thought the other would enjoy. Maybe it was a homemade loaf of bread, or a handmade lap quilt, or maybe an abstract painting. It could be a box of chocolates or a big Hershey's Kiss. It might even be a notebook and pen.

I took what each personality was like and found a gift I knew my friend would enjoy.

Years back I received the most humble of all gifts. It wasn't a Christmas or birthday gift. It was just an "I love you" gift from my youngest son, Blake.

He gave me a plain limestone rock. Its smooth surface was cool, and there was a slight groove on one side where my thumb sat comfortably. It became my worry rock. I would hold it and stroke my thumb up and down its smooth, cool surface whenever I was reading or thinking: about my book and its plots and conflicts, about finances, or about life in general. A simple item, a simple thing, became a favorite possession of mine.

Does anyone see Christmas like that? Does their heart shout and sing with joy or fret and worry during that time? It's a simple time in the year that celebrates the simple birth of our Savior—a simple man who is King of kings, Lord of lords, the rock of our salvation.

Simple, sometimes, is the greatest of all.

Day Sixteen

SACRIFICE

And all his acquaintance, and the women that followed him from
Galilee, stood afar off, beholding these things.

Luke 23:49

MY MOM HAS SO MANY stories from her childhood that she shared with me and my siblings. She was a sharecropper's child, a middle child of ten children. She may have grown up in a poor household, so poor that even a Christmas orange was a luxury, but Mom learned that Christmas wasn't the things received. Christmas was the Love celebrated.

Have you ever made sacrifices in your life? No, not the kind like no extra cup of coffee in the morning, or letting someone have the last doughnut in the box, or giving someone a few minutes of your time when you are already running late. I'm not talking about that.

I'm talking about ridding yourself of personal belongings to prove that you are committed to an act. I'm talking about putting your dreams on the line to prove that you have faith. I'm talking about giving God room.

I learned about that expression not too long ago. Over twenty-odd years ago, Bob Pierce said those words to Franklin Graham. You go as far as humanly possible and the rest is God-room—where He finishes it because it was His plan all along.

Months ago I found a book at the Tupelo Flea Market, *Rebel With a Cause*, by Franklin Graham. It was his autobiography, and I would admit that the spirit of a rebel attracts me—probably because I harbor the same spirit. I do not like to conform and will buck against it every time. I do not like to be told what to do, and sometimes will go out of my way to do the opposite. I crave adventure and excitement. I love to live life.

What kept me from going overboard? For one thing, I am not ready to die—at least not yet. I have learned that I really don't like to disappoint my Lord. And I do fear the repercussions if I rebel too much. There is the safe rebel and the extreme rebel. I am the safe rebel.

What is my cause?

As I read Franklin's story, I realized that God has a purpose for everyone. If we stop and truly listen, then we will hear it. Sometimes that purpose is to be shared; sometimes it is made to stay silent for a while.

A time will come when my purpose will blaze a trail in this world. God gave me gifts, and I can use those gifts to better myself, to make my life easier—or I could use those gifts for His Glory. To me, it's a no-brainer.

To use my gifts, sacrifices had to be made of things that held me back, hindered my dreams, my goals, my purpose. If it didn't help accomplish glorifying God's name, then why keep it?

I gave God room, and to me it was a worthy sacrifice.

Day Seventeen

FOLLOW ME

Now is my soul troubled; and what shall I say? Father, save me
from this hour: but for this cause came I unto this hour. Father,
glorify thy name. Then came there a voice from heaven, saying, I
have both glorified it, and will glorify it again.

John 12:27-28

WOULD I LEAVE MY MOTHER to follow Him? Would I cast aside
my worldly ways and treasures to follow Him? Would I trust that
He would see to my every need as I followed Him?

Would I move from my hometown, sell my home, pack my belongings, and go where He leads me? Sometimes to test my resolve
and my trust in Him, God will ask a lot of me.

I will follow Him wherever He leads me, no matter what anyone says. I asked to be His light. He showed me how. The first step
was patience. I knew where to go, and now I wait for Him to show
me how to get there.

Am I afraid? Yes. It's possible to be afraid and still trust in Him. This is a new adventure and my tour guide is my Lord.

Life once had the tendency to fill my head with all sorts of things: what would tomorrow hold? Did I spur my children far enough along in their work? Would my books sell? Would I be able to move? Would I love?

The questions kept bouncing around and worrying me. They could have driven me insane if not for the pearl of wisdom: cast your worries away.

Like a leaf on the river, all my worries would just float away. There was no need for me to worry. God would always provide what I needed most at that particular time. God would see to my heart's desire. It wasn't worldly desires for which I wished. It was more emotional and spiritual desires.

To calm my mind and help me along in my journey, I started a prayer journal. Before I began, I would wait and let a verse pop into my head: name of book, chapter, and verse. I would then open to that page and fill in two sheets of the notebook with that verse. By the end of the second page, there were no more thoughts, no more worries. My mind was calm and at peace. Things were clear.

I no longer have a prayer journal. My days end in reading God's word, talking to Him, and always trusting Him. But when I said I would follow Him, He guided me through lots and lots of steps and continues to mold me.

"In thee, O Lord, do I put my trust; let me never be ashamed: deliver me in thy righteousness" (Psalm 31:1).

Day Eighteen

PASSAGES OF TIME

*Let us break their bands asunder, and cast away their cords
from us.*

Psalm 2:1

HOW FAR WILL I GO to chase down my dreams? What will be the limit of my endurance? What will I be willing to do, to release, or to be, in order to reach that dream?

Could I follow that forever highway? What if that forever highway to my dreams called for sacrifices that I never thought possible? Would I still chase down my dream?

It is possible to put aside my fears and uncertainties when I know for certain that God is in control. He is not a God of fear or loneliness or hate. When I dedicated my life to Him, He called on me to follow Him in the most unexpected way.

Words and colors are my world. And God barraged me with a boatload of scriptures one night.

"But if any man love God, the same is known of him" (1 Corinthians 8:3).

"And whatsoever ye shall ask in my name, that will I do, that the Father may be glorified in the Son" (John 14:13).

"For we walk by faith, not by sight" (2 Corinthians 5:7).

"And Jesus, when he had found a young ass, sat thereon; as it is written, Fear not, daughter of Sion: behold, thy King cometh, sitting on an ass's colt" (John 12:14-15).

"Thou therefore endure hardness, as a good soldier of Jesus Christ" (2 Timothy 2:3).

"In him was life, and the life was the light of men" (John 1:4).

"Jesus answered and said unto her, Whosoever drinketh of this water shall thirst again: But whosoever drinketh of the water that I shall give him shall never thirst; but the water that I shall give him shall be in him a well of water springing up into everlasting life" (John 4:13-14).

"I thank my God upon every remembrance of you" (Philippians 1:3).

"Among whom also we all had our conversation in times past in the lusts of our flesh, fulfilling the desires of the flesh and of the mind; and were by nature the children of wrath, even as others" (Ephesians 2:3).

"'For I know the thoughts that I think toward you, saith the Lord, thoughts of peace, and not of evil, to give you an expected end" (Jeremiah 29:11).

"And the disciples did as Jesus had appointed them; and they made ready the passover" (Matthew 26:19).

"And he arose, and rebuked the wind, and said unto the sea, Peace, be still. And the wind ceased, and there was a great calm" (Mark 4:39).

"And he saith unto them, Follow me, and I will make you fishers of men" (Matthew 4:19).

"Blessed is the man that walketh not in the counsel of the ungodly, nor standeth in the way of sinners, nor sitteth in the seat of the scornful. But his delight is the law of the Lord, and in his law doth he meditate day and night. And he shall be like a tree planted by the rivers of water, that bringeth forth his fruit in his season; his leaf also shall not wither; and whatsoever he doeth shall prosper. The ungodly are not so: but are like the chaff which the wind driveth away. Therefore the ungodly shall not stand in the judgment, nor sinners in the congregation of the righteous. For the Lord knoweth the way of the righteous: but the way of the ungodly shall perish" (Psalm 1:1-6).

I realized that night that God was rewiring my heart.

Day Nineteen

FULL COAT OF ARMOR

Because strait is the gate, and narrow is the way,
which leadeth unto life, and few there be that find it.

Matthew 7:14

AS CHILDREN OF GOD WE are promised the desires of our hearts. At times I truly didn't know what I desired. Sometimes the things I desired were not really what I wanted or needed.

If a recent struggle in my life was a test, then my grade was a big, fat "F." I viewed myself with disgust, anger, bitterness, and disappointment—not because I fell, but because I took the grace Jesus gave me and threw it in His face. I let evil pervade my heart for a short time and allowed sin to overcome me. I knew what I was doing. I fought what I was doing. I gave in through my weakness, because I refused to kneel for strength. The devil took the past and haunted me with it, knowing the weak spots in my shield.

The world seemed out of sync. How could I go forth? How could I return to grace? How could I ask for forgiveness knowing it wasn't deserved? I could answer these with textbook questions, but not with my heart—and my silent cries became words for God to hear.

I needed His guidance. I needed to strengthen those spots in my armor, make it harder, make it more durable. I had to learn more about His Word. I had to discipline myself—but I grew weary with each passing day.

My desires were catching up with me, and I had to re-evaluate my life. I had to re-evaluate my true desires. Like a double-helix, my desire was in tandem with God's desire for me. My desire in life had to bring glory to God's name and not my own.

I may not view myself ready for His will. God knew that as a human I would fall sometimes, but His Grace set me back onto my feet, and His love gently guided me along the road.

It's with the full coat of God's armor that I travel.

Day Twenty

GAMBLING WITH GOD

My soul is weary of my life; I will leave my complaint upon my-
self; I will speak in the bitterness of my soul.

Job 10:1

I NEVER THOUGHT MY PROBLEM was pride, but it was pride
that kept me from praying for strength. It took time, but God, in
His infinite grace, healed the stain on my heart. It was a hard thing
to endure, but in the end it was worth it.

A few years back, I had been alone, without a church family, without a church, without a Bible study group. I was deeply
wounded by a former church and its unwillingness to help my family when we were struggling—struggling not only with finances
and how I was going to pay the next batch of bills, but also struggling to figure out from where the next meal would come. By this
time, I had already let the yard work go by the wayside. It didn't
matter any longer that I owned the first ever Mississippian jungle.

It didn't matter any longer that I had a larger-than-a-Volkswagen anthill just feet from the house. My main concern was what we were going to eat—what tomorrow would hold.

For too long of a time I felt ignored. I grew bitter. I felt no one cared. Bitterness grew even more, bitterness that buried the hurt deep down.

I loved that church. I grew up in that church. I was married in that church. I dedicated my children to God in that church. And I grew apart from that church.

It wasn't hard to do when I felt the false labels slapped onto me: adulteress, heathen, sinner, fornicator, etc. It hurt to see the accusing stares. It hurt to see that people believed the worst about me. Why didn't they ask how these things happened in my life? Or why? Or at the very least, why had they not been a mentor to me when it was needed most?

My hurt and my anger grew even more. I longed for my church's acceptance and love. I longed for the fellowship. And I made God a deal.

The former pastor was gone, so I doubted the new pastor would care about me. I thought this was a deal I could win.

"Lord, I will not step a foot inside that church again unless that new pastor comes and sees me first."

A month passed, and then another. I still longed for a church, a church family, the acceptance and fellowship. I still longed for a Bible study with fellow Christians. I prayed constantly and forgot about my deal with God.

But God didn't forget.

One day the pastor and his wife came to my house to visit. Their personalities meshed well with mine. And I felt the Christian love that radiated from them. God kept His end of the bargain, and I kept mine. I went to church.

I may be at a new church now, but I still have a friendship with the pastor and his wife. And I learned to never gamble with God and think I would win. He holds the ultimate hand; He holds the Royal Flush.

Day Twenty-One

NO SUCH THING
AS "THE END"

*Trust in the Lord with all thine heart; and lean not unto thine
own understanding.*

Proverbs 3:5

NO MATTER HOW I PRAYED, no matter that I conversed with
God and only got "Peace, be still," sometimes sleep eluded me.
When sleep finally found me around 3 a.m., it was usually a fitful
sleep, full of worries, of haunted dreams. It was so light a sleep that
I would be aware that I was sleeping.

When I awoke from those nights, I suffered from a migraine,
my eyes were gritty, my face was swollen from lack of sleep. One
particular night stood out among the rest, because when I awoke, it
was to the realization that I no longer wanted to be reminded that

I was a widow. I became tired of it because of the stigma that came with widowhood.

A piece was missing from my life. When things broke, I learned to fix them: ripped flooring, broken faucet, lawnmower, even the washer. My oldest son learned to do handy-man jobs: clearing brush, cutting grass, and fixing the ratty lawnmower. He helped raise his brother. My youngest son learned to keep the yard clean, fix small things like loose strips on the wall and corners, clean the fireplace, take care of the pets, and fold clothes. Both of my boys learned how to cook, and they enjoyed it.

That day I read a post by Kit Hinkle from "A Widow's Might," and two passages of the blog jumped out at me:

> Walking the path of widowhood is like being picked up every morning by a gigantic invisible hand, as though I'm one of those tiny people in *Gulliver's Travels,* and being gently plopped on the ground at the foot of the cross. Few other trials in life are so long lasting. It's there with you for years to come, with all the implications of having to brace life alone hitting you every day.

> Sister, learn to turn to Him sooner. Teach your children to acknowledge why they beg for certain things they lost from their daddy and be real that it's a loss. Don't try to jump to fix it all for them, and don't jump to try and fix your own missing pieces. Sometimes just being real that it's tough going without what you lost is the first steps to turning to God to fill in those missing pieces (http://www.awidowsmight.org/2012/01/missing-pieces).

I realized then that I did try to fill in those missing pieces. That wasn't my job. That was and still is God's job. I did pray at times for someone to share my life with, but I knew God would bring me and that man together and in a way that I would know it's a true relationship.

Until that day came, I patiently waited and continued to learn from His wisdom.

Day Twenty-Two

TEMPTATIONS OF
A WOMAN

*Unto the pure all things are pure; but unto them that are
defiled and unbelieving is nothing pure; but even their mind and
conscience is defiled.*

Titus 1:15

DID ANYONE UNDERSTAND THAT I did not want ten or even twenty friends handing out compliments, but I wanted that *one* who would find my klutziness endearing and my caterwauling in the shower charming?

Maybe it was normal for singles to feel this way. I would shout in my head (because shouting at the top of my lungs would have put me in a padded room), "Pick me! Please, just someone pick me!"

After a while I started to wonder, "*Am* I beautiful?," "Is there something wrong with me?," "Have I become undesirable?"

Thinking this way could have led me into three traps:

Promiscuity.

It's easy to give in sexually when I ache to no longer be alone. It made me feel beautiful when I was desired by another. Of course, the media spurs along this type of behavior with programs that show me how to seduce, and that one-night stands are normal and accepted in today's culture. After a while, this type of behavior would have led to even more emptiness. The physical ache would have been satisfied, but the emotional and spiritual longing would intensify.

Pretending to be someone I'm not.

It would seem so easy to transform into what another wants in a soul mate. I could assimilate his likes and hobbies. I may change my clothing style and my appearance. After a while, though, physical attraction would fade into the distance, the truth would come out, and the relationship would fall apart. Lesson: Be who I am, because it is who I am that makes me unique.

"I don't care."

Rejection after rejection came. I was ignored or forgotten. I started to feel like I would never look good enough. Why bother anymore? Eventually I would let myself go, or maybe develop an abrasive attitude. Why did I do this? My fear of rejection caused me to push away anyone so that I would never be hurt.

All three of these traps have only one destination: loneliness.

It is normal for someone to desire love, to desire companionship, and to desire a sexual relationship. As a book I read stated, "Our hearts are pulled with a strong gravitational pull towards the joy of love. Furthermore, God has clearly affirmed that there is no greater power or gift in this life than love" (Sharp 2011, 93).

When searching for that soul mate/love, I had laid down perimeters and statistics. He must have this, be like that, look like this, enjoy that, and so forth. I would pray incessantly. Eventually the "perfect" mate would come along, only for me to find out that my idea of what I wanted did not mesh with what God wanted for me.

The Bible speaks about marriage, it speaks about love; but being single, that did not soothe my soul. So where was my hope?

It was simply this: I basked in the love that Jesus gave me. I affirmed my vow to grow spiritually and remain sexually pure. I would be tempted. The world would laugh and mock me.

Everyone deserves to have someone in their life who can accept every flaw, every virtue, every quirk within us. That *someone* should be someone who puts Jesus foremost in his life. If he honors the Lord Jesus Christ, then he will honor you.

I must be content with today—then tomorrow.

I can trust Jesus with my heart.

For someone to be in my future, I had to trust Jesus. Jesus would find someone He trusted with my heart. Anyone less than that would not be worthy of my love.

And I am glad that I waited on the Lord.

Day Twenty-Three

NO VALENTINE

A man that hath friends must shew himself friendly:
and there is a friend that sticketh closer than a brother.

Proverbs 18:24

THERE WERE NO CHOCOLATES THAT year. There were no flowers, either. There was no special candle-lit dinner or restaurant meal.

What did St. Valentine's Day offer me that year? Three verses about love.

"A new commandment I give unto you, that ye love one another; as I have loved you, that ye also love one another. By this shall all men know that ye are my disciples, if ye have love one to another" (John 13:34-35).

"Owe no man anything, but to love one another: for he that loveth another hath fulfilled the law" (Romans 13:8).

"Beloved, let us love one another: for love is of God; and every one that loveth is born of God, and knoweth God" (1 John 4:7).

Then there were two books I read during that time: *Running Down Your Dreams*, by Joseph Sharp, and *Unbound*, by Neal Lozano.

"I believe that God brings us together in life with certain people, even if temporarily, to teach each other meaningful life lessons. Sometimes this includes bringing both people together to grow and change simultaneously as God's sovereignty is orchestrated throughout. Who can you reach out to in the name of love?" (Sharp 2011, 168).

"The person He sent your way is perfectly picked so that you can be an instrument of God's love for them, but also so that you can be instructed" (Lozano 2010, 158).

The excerpts were only a portion of what was written, but those two stood foremost in my mind. And I wondered that night, what could I do for others? What could I do to show my love for them?

When the word "love" was said or written, what did I think of? Did I think of love that a man and woman have for each other? Love that a parent has for a child? Or maybe love I have for another as I follow Christ? How about the love that God has for me? There were so many variations of love . . .

There was no significant other in my life at that time to whom to give a token of love; but there were my sons and my friends. It took an hour to find the perfect Hallmark e-card for my sons, but I eventually found one that expressed my love for them—in the form of Snoopy typing a poem. It took another hour to weed through the kissy-kissy, lovey-dovey, huggy-huggy e-cards to find the right one for my friends.

I finally found one. And the e-card expressed the following: "No one has a heart as big as yours." The seven people who received my e-card were people who had touched my life in some profound way. It could have been an e-mail sent on a day I needed a smile; an e-mail that encouraged me; an e-mail that led me deeper into my walk with Jesus; maybe even an hour-plus phone call that eased my soul, gave me hope, or directed me along a new path.

God placed them in my path and me in theirs so we could encourage one another, learn from one another, and lead one another. Truly, I am blessed to have received such friends. Blessings come in all forms: some for a season, some for a lifetime.

Day Twenty-Four

RAIN OF BLESSINGS

For the eyes of the Lord are over the righteous,
and his ears are open unto their prayers: but the face of the
Lord is against them that do evil.

1 Peter 3:12

LIFE SEEMED TO HAVE FOUND a way to interfere. I was so caught up in the spinning carousel that I had almost missed the good things God had done in my life—and God had indeed done good things.

The year I pledged my life to God for Him to use me for His glory, I heard "Peace, be still." I had my own style of nightly devotions. My heart was being prepared. The calm came when I gave my heart, my life, my dreams, and my desire to God. I laid my dreams and desires at my Lord's feet. I plucked that last longing out of my heart and placed it in His hands. I gave Him my all.

That was when the most amazing things started happening.

I discovered a love, someone whom I knew the Lord trusted with my heart. I found a loving and wonderful church, one that lifted its voice in praise and glory to the Lord.

My life had been one blessing after another. I had gone to Panama City, Florida for a book signing. Although I sold only one book, I knew when I met the woman who bought it for her daughter that I was there for that reason. Even though I drove home with no money in my pocket, I knew that God would provide, strengthen, and make a way for me. And He did.

No money for food? I gave it to God.

No money for gas? I gave it to God.

Through a prayer request where I had only asked for prayer, I received from another money for food. Through the cleaning of my closets and rooms, the children and I found twenty dollars' worth of coins for gas.

When I gave it to God, I learned then that once given, I couldn't take it back, and most importantly, I was completely and wholly trusting God. He filled me with His Love. He guided me in His way and the path He set before me. And He promised I wouldn't travel this alone as I had once feared.

Blessings rained down when I gave it all to God.

I feel the rain, I feel the rain
falling down on me.
I feel the rain, I feel the rain
falling down on me.

It's the former and the latter put together,
I'm not talking about the weather.
It's the Holy Ghost and it's raining down on me.

(author unknown)

Day Twenty-Five

WITH ME ALWAYS

"In the beginning was the Word, and the Word was with God,
and the Word was God."

John 1:1

NO MATTER HOW TOUGH THINGS had been—struggling to put food on the table with one part-time income in the household, wondering if the leak in the shower would ever be fixed, or if the duct work that collapsed would ever be repaired, or if the walls would ever be painted after scraping off the mold—I realized that all that was part of life and part of owning a home.

So many people give up, and I am left wondering, *why?* Maybe they didn't have the faith to trust in the One Whom I trust. Or maybe they believed that it wasn't worth the fight any longer. I could analyze it, categorize it, but not truly understand it. I could even write about it. I've been there, experienced the pain, the heartache, the worry, the desolation, and even the loneliness.

Life wanted to beat me down, smack me around, and stomp on me. But each time I found the beauty in things around me: the unconditional love of a pet that walks by my side, the fuzzy fluffiness of my bunny who loves to be petted and chased, the sing-song of the parakeets, the blueness of the sky, the sparkle of water, whether a mud puddle or in a bath tub, the laughter of my boys and my husband, even the silence of the house as we finally settle down to sleep.

The next month or next year we may not have a house or land. Come next month or next year we may not have food or a car. I have to remind myself, "Why worry?"

For every door that closes, another one opens. And each time life wants to interfere with my world, my writing, my dreams, and my life, one scripture comes to mind—a scripture that reminds me that not only do I write and live to bring glory to His Name, but I am never walking this world alone.

" . . . lo, I am with you always, even unto the end of the world."
(Matthew 28:20)

Day Twenty-Six

WAR OF THE WORDS

When I was a child, I spake as a child, I understood as a child,
I thought as a child: but when I became a man,
I put away childish things. For now we see through a glass, darkly;
but then face to face: now I know in part; but then shall I know
even as also I am known.

1 Corinthians 13:11-12

THROUGH AN E-MAIL LOOP THERE was a great discussion about what we read and what we don't read, and the hithertos and where-fores and whatnots. It had me thinking: do people truly watch what they read? Do they even care? Or do they compromise or make excuses? How did I perceive reading? What was I reading?

To me the above scripture explained it well. I may still noodle over the second half of that part, but eventually the understanding will dawn.

When I was a child, I read as a child. As I grew older, I developed a more literary and complex reading pattern. Spiritually I was still a child. Now that I am more mature in my spiritual walk with Jesus, I have done away with childish things, with immature things. I have a more mature palate for reading.

Good books are found in both worlds, the Christian and the secular. Horrible books are found in both worlds, the Christian and the secular. The key to my dilemma on what to read and what to keep was this: what would Jesus read?

I've read Christian books that pushed the language barrier or pushed the scenes a bit too far for comfort. Too many authors must think they need to push the line to be "more real" or to "reach out to others."

The closer the walk with Jesus, the more I stayed away from that which is of this world. The more I love Jesus, the more the world hated me. I would rather build up my rewards in Heaven than in this world. I would rather have beautiful and praiseworthy books, Christian and secular, than trite, preachy, erotic or vulgar books. To know the difference in what to read and what to write, discernment is the key. To gain discernment, prayer is needed. To gain prayer, I must talk with Jesus on a daily basis.

Why would I defile myself with words that Jesus would not like when I could read so many books that would bring honor and glory to His name or reach out to the hurting, lonely, and lost?

Why be a stumbling block to another? If a person is trying to curb cursing, why give a book with cursing in it? If a person is trying to put away a past memory of assault, then why give a book with a descriptive scene of such an assault? If a person is trying to break the bond of sexual promiscuity, then why give a book with sex scenes?

Two verses help me with choosing what to read and what not to read, and more importantly, what to write and what not to write:

> "Finally, brethren, whatsoever things are true, whatsoever things are honest, whatsoever things are just, whatsoever things are pure, whatsoever things are lovely, whatsoever things are of good report; if there be any virtue, and if there be any praise, think on these things" (Philippians 4:8).

> "But those things which proceed out of the mouth come forth from the heart; and they defile the man" (Matthew 15:18).

Day Twenty-Seven

CHRIST OR THE WORLD

Love not the world, neither the things that are in the world. If any man love the world, the love of the Father is not in him. For all that is in the world, the lust of the flesh, and the lust of the eyes, and the pride of life, is not of the Father, but is of the world. And the world passeth away, and the lust thereof: but he that doeth the will of God abideth forever.

1 John 2:15-17

ONE DAY I RECEIVED A beautiful e-mail from a lady in Australia who wanted to help me. She felt led to help me, and a verse stayed with her the whole time while praying.

"If a brother or sister be naked, and destitute of daily food, And one of you say unto them, Depart in peace, be ye warmed and filled; notwithstanding ye give them not those things which are needful to the body; what doth it profit? Even so faith, if it hath not works, is dead, being alone" (James 2:15-17).

This was the face of Christianity: a sister in Christ reaching beyond continental boundaries to help another sister in Christ. This world is for a short time, but my eternal destination is . . . well, for eternity.

Another face of Christianity was the willingness to stand for Christ and to never compromise or conform to the world.

Facebook and other social media outlets have become a battle ground for many people. Sometimes I get swept along in the battle wave. Someone would stand for their beliefs, either on one side or the other, or that someone would sit on the sidelines or straddle the line. If I stand for Christ, there is no middle line for me. It's an all-or-nothing stance. I would stand for all that He teaches and commands—not just the parts about love, but also the parts about hell and sin, about the hatred of the world against those who follow Him, and the narrow path that all followers must walk.

I cannot simply say I have a deep faith in Christ and support issues that go against his teachings. I cannot say that I have Christ within me and then support homosexuality, indoctrination of Muslim teachings in school, prosecution and oppression of conservative Christian worship, and the list goes on.

As a Christian, I realized I am attacked by my own people, my own government, and my own brothers and sisters. I cannot be of this world and of Christ at the same time. I have to make a stand. In love, and not judging or condemning those who sin and support sin, I should show that if they don't turn from the world then Hell is their destination.

And when I am attacked even more for my beliefs, I shall remember the verse from Luke:

"And whosoever will not receive you, when ye go out of that city, shake off the very dust from your feet for a testimony against them" (Luke 9:5).

Day Twenty-Eight

DECLUTTERING

For it is easier for a camel to go through a needle's eye,
than for a rich man to enter into the Kingdom of God.

Luke 18:25

I HAVE READ A BOOK titled *Declutter Now!* that revealed a lot of hidden wisdom and quiet revelations throughout the pages. As I started this book, I only made it through a few chapters when I realized how potent these words were.

It wasn't about the clutter within the home. It was more than that.

As I made my declutter list, I realized that my home was the physical representation of my life. Somewhere along the line in the last two years, I allowed "things" to clutter my home and my life.

I started in the bathroom closet, the smallest area in my house, and eventually finished with the laundry room, the most crowded area in my house. As my family decluttered, we filled box after box with clothes, shoes, hats, and coats. There were books, art supplies, and dishes. A lot of the items were actually trash. I mean, who needed ten non-working pens or five stubby pencils or dried up modeling clay?

All these things, all this clutter, could have been thrown out or given away months ago. Instead, it took up space in my home. These things created barriers that we had to wade through to reach our goal, be it a pot at the back of the cabinet, the favorite coffee mug, or a working pen.

Now the rooms were neat and clean. The house was navigable. As the space lightened in my home, I felt it lighten in my soul.

My house had become cluttered because my soul had become cluttered.

Worry, fear, wishes, aggravation, longing, and distractions made their way to the forefront of my life. I shouldn't have worried about tomorrow. What should I fear? Aggravation shouldn't have hampered me. My longing is known to God, so why dwell on it? And distractions were just that: distractions to keep me from looking at the clutter in my life so that I would not be able to fix it.

Sorry, devil. The game was up. I saw the distraction, I saw the clutter, and I conquered them.

With the clutter in my home and the clutter in my life, it kept me from doing what I had always felt God wanted me to do: to follow my dreams and write my stories. So many barriers and so many obstacles had gotten in the way, preventing me.

I saw them for what they were: material things that will never go with me into Heaven.

Less is more, as it says in the book.

With less in my life, I could focus on the important things: my husband, my kids, my pets, my dreams, and God's word.

Day Twenty-Nine

ONE MAMA'S STORY

Thou therefore endure hardness, as a good soldier of Jesus Christ.

2 Timothy 2:3

THE CHRISTMAS ORANGE **BY BETTY** Sue Tutor:

I grew up in a large family. As a large, poor family we seldom had a Christmas tree, much less Christmas toys. We waited for Santa Claus, but usually we got an orange and a note promising presents "next year." The Christmas that always stood out in my mind was when I was around three years old.

I remember waking up on Christmas morning and seeing a lot of cars and trucks in the yard. We didn't own a vehicle, so even a few cars would seem like a lot to me back then. We had just moved into the community and had very few household items. I remember walking into a room that must have been a living room without furniture, and there were several people sitting around on the floor with boxes of food, toys, presents, fruit, and clothes in front of them.

My mom was sitting in a straight-back chair holding the baby, and someone asked, "Which one is Betty Sue?" My older sister pushed me towards the person, but I was reluctant to go as I was a very shy child. My mom encouraged me to go to them. The person who asked for me showed me a box with my name on it and said it was for me. The one thing that caught my eye was an orange. I grabbed the orange and bit into the peeling. Nothing else mattered but that orange.

The people who came that Christmas morning were from a local church. And they had heard of a poor family that had a lot of kids without a Christmas . . . and that was the best Christmas I ever had.

This memory had helped me understand missionaries, missions, and the true meaning of Christmas. These people were simple ordinary people going about the Lord's work, and none of them knew the impact they had on my life nor the influence they had on me as a Christian.

I shared this memory with my mom and older sister when I was eighteen years old. They were both surprised I could remember that Christmas, since I was only three years old. My mom filled me in on the circumstances: how the church had heard from the farmer, on whose land we were living, about how we were poor, without food and without winter clothes. She said she cried that day thanking God for sending these people to help us and told me to keep this memory, to share it with my kids . . . I did, and I have.

Every Christmas I look forward to my Christmas orange, and every Christmas I find my orange under the tree, even if I have to put it there myself on Christmas Eve. A bag of oranges can sit on my counter, but the one that tastes the best is the one I find under the Christmas tree on Christmas morning.

Praise God for ordinary people willing to go about doing the Lord's work, and thank God for Christmas morning and my Christmas orange.

Day Thirty

IN MEMORY OF PUDDIN

*For God so loved the world He gave his only begotten
Son that whosoever believeth in Him should not perish
but have everlasting life.*

John 3:16

BELOW IS ANOTHER CHRISTMAS STORY told by my mother and in memory of my Aunt Puddin (Mary Jane McGregory), who died April 1, 2010.

The Christmas Gift I Will Never Forget by Betty Sue Tutor:

At some point in everybody's life, they will get a gift that will last a lifetime—if not the gift, at least the memory. I received such a gift from my older sister, Puddin, when I was about fifteen years old.

Puddin and I fought over her dresses, shirts, skirts, pants, and shorts, but never shoes—I didn't care for shoes.

I wore her clothes every chance I got, not because I didn't have any of my own, but simply because I could, because they fit, and because it was my way of showing the world that I did it. I finally caught up with her; now I was as big as she was.

There was one item of clothing that I knew she would never rip off of me, and that was a yellow dress. It was a golden yellow dress with a pleat down the front. Even though I didn't like the color yellow, I loved that dress. I liked the way it fit, liked the way it felt, and loved the way it made me feel when I wore it.

And wear it I did, every time it was washed. I would volunteer to iron it. Afterwards, I'd hang it in the closet behind everything else so I could find it first. I'd get up early the next morning, before Puddin did, and I'd put on that dress. She would get mad. She would call me names. She did everything she could to get me to leave her dress alone.

Then one December day I couldn't find the yellow dress. It didn't matter that it was short-sleeved. I would wear it spring, summer, fall or winter if it was clean. I wanted to wear it on the last day of school before Christmas break. I wanted to wear it on Christmas Day, but I couldn't find it anywhere. I even looked in Mama's closet.

I gave up. The last day of school came and went. Then Christmas Eve came, and I still couldn't find that dress. So on Christmas morning, instead of the dress that made me feel so good, I put on regular clothes.

We opened our gifts. We oohed and aahed over our presents and our surprises, over one another's presents and surprises, but there was one present left under the tree.

I wondered why I hadn't seen that rectangular box before, like the day before Christmas when I had shaken or squeezed every gift under the tree to see if I could figure out what they were. My first thought was that if I had known that present was under the tree I could have cut the tape and opened it, and no one would have known. I shrugged and waited for someone to open the present.

Then Puddin picked up the gift, handed it to me, and said, "Merry Christmas." I never figured she would give me a Christmas present unless she drew my name—I was that much of a brat.

Nervously, I unwrapped the box, not knowing what was going on. Was this her way of getting revenge? Was this her way of embarrassing me after all those years? I opened the box with everyone watching.

I looked down and there it was—the yellow dress; the yellow dress I searched the house for; the yellow dress that made me feel so good. I thanked her. I even hugged her neck. I hung it up in the closet and couldn't wait until school started again so I could wear that yellow dress.

She was as surprised as me. She thought I would get mad at her for giving me a "used" gift. I told her no. That was the best Christmas gift she could have given me.

I will always remember that yellow dress. I wore that dress in one of my school pictures. It was never passed down. I didn't outgrow it like the other dresses. I literally wore it out. Even though I haven't kept that dress, I have kept the memory.

It's a memory I've shared with my kids, and now I share with their kids. To Puddin it was a "used" gift, but to me it was the best Christmas gift I got that year. To me it was the gift I will never forget.

AFTERWORD

THE LAST TWO STORIES ARE my mother's. She always told these to us, and so many more. I really should have a book devoted to the life of Betty Sue, but until then I make do with reading about her memories.

Her Christmas orange story helped to make sense of why every Christmas we had an orange. And no other orange would smell as sweet, taste as soothing, and feel as smooth as that Christmas orange.

When I read the story of the yellow dress, I realized that was probably one of the many reasons why my siblings and I grew up appreciating the small and simple things in life. We never fell into the trap of "keeping up with the Joneses."

Her stories and teachings I have never forgotten, and I used them to raise my own children. So, thank you, Mom. Thank you for the spankings, the groundings, the yelling, the adventures, the smiles, the hugs—but thank you especially for the love you gave me.

My spiritual journey is not over—not by a long shot. I honestly believe it will never be over. Someday I might realize I let pride or bitterness back in, or I let my fears and self-loathing pervade me.

Someday I might actually acquire my one luxury item or fulfill one dream only to realize that there is another.

Life is a journey. And I am eager to travel it with my Lord.

I pray that this book has helped you in some form or fashion. May God bless your dreams and bless your life.

Daphne

BIBLIOGRAPHY

Gerke, Jeff. *The Art & Craft of Writing Christian Fiction*. Colorado Springs: Marcher Lord Press, 2009.

Graham, Franklin. *Rebel With a Cause*. Nashville: Thomas Nelson, 1995.

Hinkle, Kit. "Missing Pieces: How Children Crave What They Lost." January 6, 2012, http://www.awidowsmight.org.

Lozano, Neal. *Unbound: A Practical Guide to Deliverance*. Grand Rapids: Chosen Books, 2010.

McGhee, Robert S. *The Search for Significance*. Nashville: Thomas Nelson, 2003.

Ridpath, Ian. *Astronomy*. New York: DK Publishing, 2006.

Sharp, Joseph W. *Running Down Your Dreams*. Peoria: Intermedia Publishing, 2011.

For more information about
D.M. Webb
&

30 Days: A Devotional Memoir
please visit:

website: www.dmwebb.com
email: dmwebb42@gmail.com
Twitter: @DaphMichele
Facebook: www.facebook.com/WebbDM
Pinterest: http://pinterest.com/rosesnbttrflies

For more information about
AMBASSADOR INTERNATIONAL
please visit:

www.ambassador-international.com
@AmbassadorIntl
www.facebook.com/AmbassadorIntl

www.ingramcontent.com/pod-product-compliance
Lightning Source LLC
Chambersburg PA
CBHW071608040426
42452CB00008B/1281